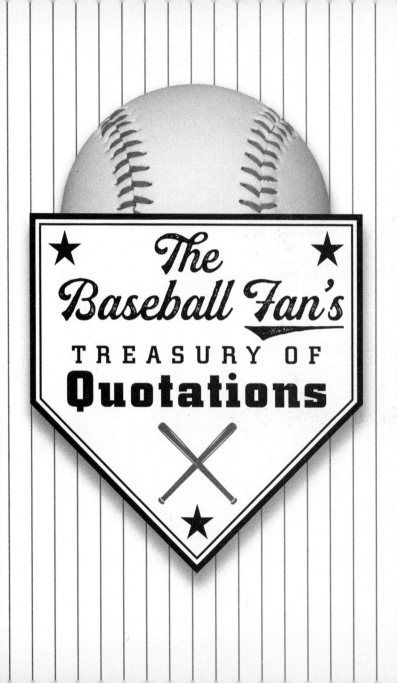

The Baseball Fan's

TREASURY OF

Quotations

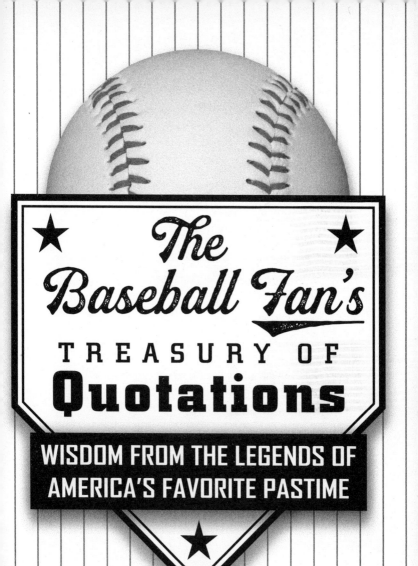

The Baseball Fan's

TREASURY OF

Quotations

WISDOM FROM THE LEGENDS OF AMERICA'S FAVORITE PASTIME

Hatherleigh Press is committed to preserving and protecting the natural resources of the earth. Environmentally responsible and sustainable practices are embraced within the company's mission statement.

Visit us at www.hatherleighpress.com and register online for free offers, discounts, special events, and more.

THE BASEBALL FAN'S TREASURY OF QUOTATIONS

Library of Congress Cataloging-in-Publication Data is available.
ISBN: 978-1-57826-750-7

DESIGN BY CAROLYN KASPER

CONTENTS

INTRODUCTION

BASEBALL OCCUPIES a special place in the American imagination. Who among us hasn't dreamt of stepping out onto the field at Dodger's Stadium, standing in the shade of the Green Monster, or getting lost in the Ivy at Wrigley?

Part of what makes baseball great is that, without fail, everyone who has ever watched a game has thought, "I could do that." It seems so plausible. So realistic. Anyone can pick up a ball and throw it, we think. Anyone can swing a bat and hold dreams of the feel of wood on leather. It's nothing special, we suppose. Playing baseball is like breathing; it can be hard sometimes, but for the most part it's almost an afterthought.

That the men who play the game professionally don't seem any different from the rest of us feeds this perception. Basketball players tower over us, and football players outweigh us, but you could pass a baseball player on the street and not even notice. Baseball players are susceptible to the same flights of fancy, the same bursts of anger, even the same hero worship as we are. These men, who are paid to live every child's dream, are no different from any of us.

This Treasury of Quotations contains the words of many a great man, but their words could have come from any one of us. They echo the emotions, the hopes and the dreams that we feel every time we hear the umpire shout, "Play ball!"

BASEBALL GAMES are serious business. From the first pitch to the final out, smiles are few and far between. But once the field clears and the teams funnel back into their respective dugouts, the tension lifts, and so do everyone's spirits. Only then does it become obvious just how much joy—and how many jokes—there are in baseball.

Okay you guys, pair up in threes!

—YOGI BERRA

It took me seventeen years to get three thousand hits in baseball. It took one afternoon on the golf course.

Had I known I was going to live this long, I'd have taken better care of myself!

—MICKEY MANTLE

They say some of my stars drink whiskey. But I have found that the ones who drink milkshakes don't win many ball games.

—FRED McMANE

If you don't think too good, don't think too much.

—TED WILLIAMS

I've never questioned the integrity of an umpire. Their eyesight, yes.

—LEO DUROCHER

How can I play baseball when I'm worried about foreign policy?

—CHARLES M SCHULTZ

Ideally, the umpire should combine the integrity of a Supreme Court judge, the physical agility of an acrobat, the endurance of Job and the imperturbability of Buddha.

—TIME-LIFE BOOKS

Don't name your kid after a ballpark. Cubs fans Paul and Teri Fields have named their newborn son Wrigley. Wrigley Fields. A child is supposed to be an independent individual, not a means of touting your own personal hobbies. At least that's what I've always taught my kids, Panama Red and Jacuzzi.

—BILL MAHER

Nobody deserves to go to the World Series more than the Chicago Cubs. But they can't go because that would spoil their custom of never going. It is an irreconcilable paradox.

—BILL BRYSON

That's why baseball is more like life than other games. Sometimes I feel like that's all I do in life, keep track of my errors.

—MICHAEL CHABON

The New York Mets are planning to move the walls of Citi Field in order to increase the number of home runs they hit. Call me old fashioned but isn't that what steroids are for?

—CONAN O'BRIEN

The Yankees have blown a 10-game lead in the standings, and are now tied for first place. You can tell they're depressed. Today, five of their players tested positive for Häagen-Dazs.

—JIMMY FALLON

To be an American and unable to play baseball is comparable to being a Polynesian and unable to swim.

—JOHN CHEEVER

Sliding headfirst is the safest way to get to the next base, I think. And the fastest. You don't lose your momentum.... And there is one more important reason that I slide headfirst. It gets my picture in the newspaper.

—PETE ROSE

The average age of our bench is deceased.

—TOMMY LASORDA

I walk into the clubhouse and it's like walking into the Mayo Clinic. We have four doctors, three therapists and five trainers. Back when I broke in, we had one trainer who carried a bottle of rubbing alcohol and by the seventh inning he had drunk it all.

—TOMMY LASORDA

Ninety percent of this game is half mental.

—YOGI BERRA

Who is this Baby Ruth? And what does she do?

—GEORGE BERNARD SHAW

The way to make coaches think you're in shape in the spring is to get a tan.

—WHITEY FORD

Running a ball club is like raising kids who fall out of trees.

—TOM TREBELHORN

I watch a lot of baseball on radio.

—GERALD FORD

I think I throw the ball as hard as anyone. The ball just doesn't get there as fast.

—EDDIE BANE

Third ain't so bad if nothin' is hit to you.

—YOGI BERRA

Bob Gibson is the luckiest pitcher I ever saw. He always pitches when the other team doesn't score any runs.

—TIM McCARVER

I never took the game home with me. I always left it in some bar.

—BOB LEMON

The other teams could make trouble for us if they win.

—YOGI BERRA

We know we're better than this, but we can't prove it.

—TONY GWYNN

Alan Sutton Sothoron pitched his initials off today.

—ANONYMOUS, ST. LOUIS
NEWSPAPER

All I remember about my wedding day in 1967 is that the Cubs lost a doubleheader.

—GEORGE F. WILL

The funny thing about these uniforms is that you hang them in the closet and they get smaller and smaller.

—CURT FLOOD

Sure I played, did you think I was born age 70 sitting in a dugout trying to manage guys like you?

—CASEY STENGEL, TO MICKEY MANTLE

There are two theories on hitting the knuckleball. Unfortunately, neither one of them works.

—CHARLIE LAU

Think! How the hell are you gonna think and hit at the same time?

—YOGI BERRA

As a nation we are dedicated to keeping physically fit—and parking as close to the stadium as possible.

—BILL VAUGHAN

A man once told me to walk with the Lord. I'd rather walk with the bases loaded.

—KEN SINGLETON

I'd be willing to bet you, if I was a betting man, that I have never bet on baseball.

—PETE ROSE

Lasorda's standard reply when some new kid would ask directions to the whirlpool was to tell him to stick his foot in the toilet and flush it.

—STEVE GARVEY

So I'm ugly. So what? I never saw anyone hit with his face.

—YOGI BERRA

Now there's three things you can do in a baseball game: You can win or you can lose or it can rain.

—CASEY STENGEL

I can remember a reporter asking me for a quote, and I didn't know what a quote was. I thought it was some kind of soft drink.

—JOE DIMAGGIO

I knew when my career was over. In 1965 my baseball card came out with no picture.

—BOB EUCKER

The Angels could take batting practice in a hotel lobby and not break the chandelier.

—BILL LEE

The coach put me in right field only because it was against the rules to put me in Sweden, where I would have done less damage to the team.

—DAVE BARRY

The 1958 Kansas City Athletics lost 81 games. That was, perhaps, the best of all the Athletics teams to play in Kansas City, though this seems a bit like saying that Cocoa Krispies is the healthiest of all the cereals that begin with the word "Cocoa."

—JOE POSNANSKI

In 1962 I was named Minor League Player of the Year. It was my second season in the bigs.

—BOB EUCKER

Miguel Olivo couldn't block the plate with a 2-foot thick concrete wall and the Indianapolis Colts offensive line.

—JOE POSNANSKI

If Mike Scioscia raced his pregnant wife he'd finish third.

—TOMMY LASORDA

It is in the field that Aoki is a particular joy to watch; I have never seen a player look so confused while making so many good plays. It is like Aoki's mind is a lost GPS voice repeating, "Still calculating."

—JOE POSNANSKI

If you don't succeed at first, try pitching.

—JACK HARSHMAN

A SWING
AND A
MISS

WHAT THE game gives, it also takes away. For every moment of joy, for every ball that lands beyond the fence in the clutches of a young child, there is a crushing ninth inning strikeout, a rally-killing double play, a long losing streak. The quotes in this chapter reflect the pain, anger, and frustration that are all so integral to the game of baseball.

You may glory in a team triumphant, but you fall in love with a team in defeat. Losing after great striving is the story of man, who was born to sorrow, whose sweetest songs tell of saddest thought, and who, if he is a hero, does nothing in life as becomingly as leaving it.

—ROGER KAHN

We picked the Red Sox because they lose. If you root for something that loses for 86 years, you're a pretty good fan. You don't have to win everything to be a fan of something.

—JIMMY FALLON

...[T]here's almost nothing worse than spending an entire day anticipating watching a Yankees vs. Red Sox game, only to have the score be 9-0 in the third inning.

—Tucker Elliot

A baseball game is simply a nervous breakdown divided into nine innings.

—Earl Wilson

Baseball is a team game but, at the same time, it's a very lonely game: unlike in soccer or basketball, where players roam around, in baseball everyone has their little plot of the field to tend. When the action comes to you, the spotlight is on you but no one can help you.

—Chad Harbach

It kills me to lose. If I'm a troublemaker, and I don't think that my temper makes me one, then it's because I can't stand losing. That's the way I am about winning, all I ever wanted to do was finish first.

—JACKIE ROBINSON

Baseball is like a poker game. Nobody wants to quit when he's losing; nobody wants you to quit when you're ahead.

—JACKIE ROBINSON

Losing feels worse than winning feels good.

—VIN SCULLY

Andre Dawson has a bruised knee and is listed as day-to-day (pause). Aren't we all?

—VIN SCULLY

Darryl Strawberry is not a dog; a dog is loyal and runs after balls.

—TOMMY LASORDA

When we win, I'm so happy I eat a lot. When we lose, I'm so depressed, I eat a lot. When we're rained out, I'm so disappointed I eat a lot.

—TOMMY LASORDA

I hate all hitters. I start a game mad and I stay that way until it's over.

—DON DRYSDALE

Don Drysdale would consider an intentional walk a waste of three pitches. If he wants to put you on base, he can hit you with one pitch.

—MIKE SHANNON

[Buck Showwalter] never even smelled a jock in the big leagues. Mr. Baseball never even got a hit in Triple-A. I was a better player than him, I have more money than him and I'm better looking than him.

—OZZIE GUILLEN

I get drunk because I'm happy we win or I get drunk because I'm very sad and disturbed because we lose. Same routine, it never changes. It's been the same routine for 25, 28 years. It doesn't change. I don't like to go out.

—Ozzie Guillen

You can't win them all.

—Connie Mack

Don't worry, the fans don't start booing until July.

—Earl Weaver

On my tombstone just write, 'The sorest loser that ever lived.'

—EARL WEAVER

We're so bad right now that for us back-to-back home runs means one today and another one tomorrow.

—EARL WEAVER

Everybody kind of perceives me as being angry. It's not anger, it's motivation.

—ROGER CLEMENS

In a world filled with hate, prejudice, and protest, I find that I too am filled with hate, prejudice, and protest.

—Bob Gibson

I had to fight all my life to survive. They were all against me, but I beat the bastards and left them in the ditch.

—Ty Cobb

Every season has its peaks and valleys. What you have to try to do is eliminate the Grand Canyon.

—Andy Van Slyke

One of the great things about baseball is there's a crisis every day.

—GABE PAUL

I don't mind getting beaten, but I hate to lose. God, I hate to lose.

—REGGIE JACKSON

If you have a bad day in baseball, and start thinking about it, you will have 10 more.

—SAMMY SOSA

Any time you think you have the game conquered, the game will turn around and punch you right in the nose.

—MIKE SCHMIDT

Some days you tame the tiger. Sometimes the tiger eats you for lunch.

—TUG McGRAW

After I hit a home run I ran the bases with my head down. I figured the pitcher felt bad enough without me showing him up.

—MICKEY MANTLE

Nobody likes to hear it, because it's dull, but the reason you win or lose is darn near always the same: pitching.

—EARL WEAVER

When I throw a curve that hangs and it goes for a hit, I want to chew up my glove.

—DON DRYSDALE

Hitting slumps like sleeping in a soft bed. Easy to get into and hard to get out of.

—JOHNNY BENCH

I don't care what they say. Winning is good...losing isn't fun. No participation trophies. First place only.

—BRYCE HARPER

If a tie is like kissing your sister, losing is like kissing your grandmother with her teeth out.

—GEORGE BRETT

The last time the Cubs won the World Series was 1908. The last time they were in one was 1945. Hey, any team can have a bad century.

—TOM TREBELHORN

You may glory in a team triumphant... But you fall in love with a team in defeat.

—ROGER KAH

Love is the most important thing in the world, but baseball is pretty good, too.

—YOGI BERRA

As long as you live keep smiling because it brightens everybody's day.

—VIN SCULLY

When the Dodgers left, it was not only a loss of a team, it was the disruption of a social pattern. A total destruction of a culture.

—Joe Flaherty

We wept, Brooklyn was a lovely place to hit. If you got a ball in the air, you had a chance to get it out. When they tore down Ebbets Field, they tore down a little piece of me.

—Duke Snider

On [Campanella's] last trip to the mound, the city of Los Angeles says hello to him. Listen.

—Vin Scully

Now he won't be suffering anymore. I loved Roy Campanella, I loved him like a brother. I'm going to miss him very much. As well as being a great baseball player, he was a great human being.

—HALL OF FAME MANAGER
TOMMY LASORDA

For the past two weeks you have been reading about a bad break I got. Yet today I consider myself the luckiest man on the face of the earth.

—LOU GEHRIG

So they unhitched the Iron Horse from the old wagon, but Marse Joe McCarthy didn't order him to be taken behind the barn and destroyed.

—JOHN KIERAN

I never knew how someone dying could say he was the luckiest man in the world. But now I understand.

—MICKEY MANTLE

I don't have kids, so hitting a HR for Jose Fernandez is the best moment of my life.

—DEE GORDON

For us, Fernandez is still alive, we see a bigger life for him. When we're at home, we look around and we see his locker, that makes you feel sad.

—JOSE URENA

[Fernandez] doesn't really go away. He's always got a place in my heart.

—DON MATTINGLY

Although he is gone, all sorts of reminders of Clemente still exist. More than anything, Roberto Clemente left behind memories of how he played the game on the field and how he lived his life off it.

—STEW THORNLEY

Crosley Field. When you came through that left field gate and saw that green grass, it was better than going to heaven.

—LOU DOLLIN

Again, the excavators rolled backward to where Mantle and Joe D and Bernie once chased fly balls. Within seconds, the section came out like a wisdom tooth extracted. The concrete portion of the roof tumbled forward, then down, followed by the risers where seats were once attached. The dust cloud dissipated quickly. Visit the Bronx on Thursday. Watch 'em take down another piece of history.

—RICHARD SANDOMIR

Not just anyone is going to get the nickname "The Captain" …There will never be another Derek Jeter, but the traits and qualities that made him special are things that I hope to pass down to younger players throughout the remainder of my career.

— DEXTER FOWLER

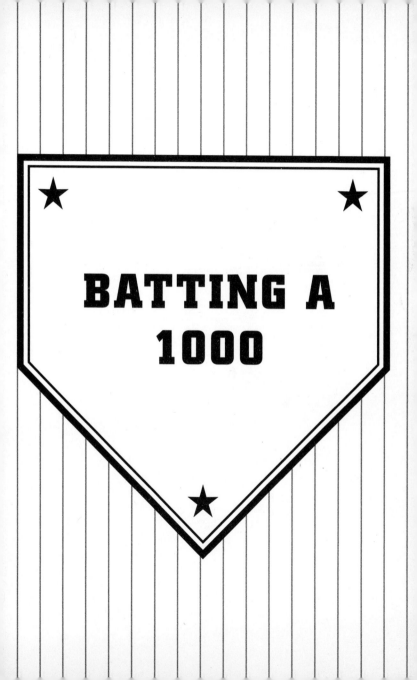

BATTING A 1000

SOCCER, BASKETBALL, and football lend themselves easily to hero worship. In baseball, by contrast, the margins are slimmer, the competition fiercer, and appreciation for one's opponents and their achievements are few and far between. Only the greatest players receive recognition from their peers.

All year long they looked to him to light the fire and all year long he answered the demands. High fly ball into right field. She is gone! In a year that has been so improbable, the impossible has happened.

—VIN SCULLY

Way back…This ball is gone!! …This crowd will not stop…They can't believe the ending… And this time, Mighty Casey did NOT strike out!

—DON DRYSDALE

Trying to hit Sandy Koufax was like trying to drink coffee with a fork.

—WILLIE STARGELL

Greg Maddux could put a baseball through a life saver if you asked him.

—Joe Morgan

When Rivera takes the mound, the other team is sitting in the dugout thinking, "We've got no chance. It's over." This guy walks into the game, and they are done.

—Rich Gossage

Fingers has thirty-five saves. Rollie has a better record than John the Baptist.

—Lon Simmons

Bob Gibson is the luckiest pitcher in baseball. He is always pitching when the other team doesn't score any runs.

—TIM MCCARVER

Every hitter likes fastballs just like everybody likes ice cream. But you don't like it when someone's stuffing it into you by the gallon. That's how you feel when Nolan Ryan's throwing balls by you.

—REGGIE JACKSON

I can throw out any man alive.

—JOHNNY BENCH

A man has to have goals. Mine was to have people say, 'There goes Ted Williams, the greatest hitter who ever lived.'

—TED WILLIAMS

Tom Glavine is like a tailor; a little off here, a little off there & you're done, take a seat.

—VIN SCULLY

Fans don't boo nobody's.

—REGGIE JACKSON

A woman will be elected President before Wade Boggs is called out on strikes. I guarantee that.

—GEORGE BRETT

Roberto Clemente could field the ball in New York and throw out a guy in Pennsylvania.

—VIN SCULLY

I was such a dangerous hitter I even got intentional walks in batting practice.

—CASEY STENGEL

I think I was the best baseball player I ever saw.

—WILLIE MAYS

Mike Trout doesn't have to care [about analytics] because he's the best at everything.

— CLAYTON KERSHAW

Blind people come to the park just to hear Tom Seaver pitch.

— REGGIE JACKSON

We are both lefties. Koufax can't pitch on Yom Kippur. I can't pitch.

— BARACK OBAMA

At times I'll be listening to Vin and I'll think, Oh, I wish I could call upon that expression the way he does. He paints the picture more beautifully than anyone who's ever called a baseball game.

—DICK ENBERG

Maddux is like a meticulous surgeon out there... he puts the ball where he wants to. You see a pitch inside and wonder, "Is it the fastball or the cutter?" That's where he's got you.

—TONY GWYNN

Every time Roger Clemens pitches it's exciting, whether it's 289 or 299. It's exciting because we're watching a guy that's going into the Hall of Fame.

—JOE TORRE

There's nobody like Ichiro in either league—now or ever. He exists strictly within his own world, playing a game 100 percent unfamiliar to everyone else.

—BRUCE JENKINS

Some people have asked me whether or not Rickey Henderson belonged in the Hall of Fame. I've replied, "If you could somehow split him in two, you'd have two Hall of Famers."

—BILL JAMES

Sandy's fastball was so fast, some batters would start to swing as he was on his way to the mound.

—JIM MURRAY

Greg Maddux was convinced no hitter could tell the speed of a pitch with any meaningful accuracy…Sometimes hitters can pick up differences in spin. They can identify pitches if there are different releases points or if a curveball starts with an upward hump as it leaves the pitcher's hand. But if a pitcher can change speeds, every hitter is helpless, limited by human vision. "Except," Maddux said, "for that [EXPLETIVE] Tony Gwynn."

—THOMAS BOSWELL

This is a general manager's dream. In baseball history, Babe Ruth was traded, Rogers Hornsby traded, and now Ken Griffey, Jr.

—CINCINNATI REDS GENERAL
MANAGER JIM BOWDEN

Lou Gehrig never learned that a ballplayer couldn't be good every day.

—HANK GOWDY

Does Pete Rose hustle? Before the All-Star game he came into the clubhouse and took off his shoes and they ran another mile without him.

—HANK AARON

With most great players on other teams, you notice how great they are, but when they become teammates and you see them every day, you notice the flaws. It is exactly the opposite with George Brett.

—JIM SUNDBERG

I can't imagine what it was like seeing Ruth, Williams, Aaron, Mays, DiMaggio, Cobb, etcetera in the prime of their careers, but somehow, it must have been like what we see Barry doing right now. He completely dominates the game, just as all the great stars of their day did.

—TOM CANDIOTTI

My idea of managing is giving the ball to Tom Seaver and sitting down and watching him work.

—SPARKY ANDERSON

If consistency is a jewel, then Mr. Hornsby is a whole rope of pearls.

—JOE WILLIAMS

I got a big charge out of seeing Ted Williams hit. Once in a while they let me try to field some of them, which sort of dimmed my enthusiasm.

—ROCKY BRIDGES

You can have your Cobbs, your Lajoies, your Chases, your Bakers, but I'll take Wagner as my pick of the greatest. He is not only a marvelous mechanical player, but he has the quickest baseball brain I have ever observed.

—JOHN MCGRAW

Mike Trout is a humble, clean-shaven baseball prodigy from a small town in southern New Jersey. He works at Angel Stadium, three and a half miles from places called Fantasyland, Tomorrowland and Main Street, U.S.A. His story springs from all of them.

—SPORTSWRITER TYLER KEPNER

No man in the history of baseball had as much power as Mickey Mantle. No man. You're not talking about ordinary power. Dave Kingman has power. Willie Mays had power. Then when you're talking about Mickey Mantle—it's an altogether different level. Separates the men from the boys.

—BILLY MARTIN

I think it's incredible because there were guys like Mays and Mantle and Aaron who were great players for ten years... I only had four or five good years.

—SANDY KOUFAX

Yogi seemed to be doing everything wrong, yet everything came out right. He stopped everything behind the plate and hit everything in front of it.

—MEL OTT

I can't believe that Babe Ruth was a better player than Willie Mays. Ruth is to baseball what Arnold Palmer is to golf. He got the game moving. But I can't believe he could run as well as Mays, and I can't believe he was any better an outfielder.

—SANDY KOUFAX

I'm not sure what the hell charisma is, but I get the feeling it's Willie Mays.

—TED KLUSZEWSKI

Palmeiro's an incredible player. He has hit all types of pitching for a long time and plays every day. He's a Hall of Famer, no doubt about it. And he's got some baseball left—he doesn't seem to be slowing down much.

—MIKE SCIOSCIA

Ortiz is bulletproof, as far as I'm concerned. Whether there's a lefthander on the mound or a right hander on the mound, he beats us up pretty good.

—JOE TORRE

When Jack first entered (the Major Leagues), there were still a lot of people who didn't know if it was the right thing to do. Pee Wee used all of his leadership skills and sensitivity to bring the team together... Pee Wee was more than a friend. Pee Wee was a good man.

—RACHEL ROBINSON

I would put him right behind Barry Bonds. I think Barry's an incredible force and their club did qualify for the playoffs. Barry had a monster season for a winning team, so I would say that he's probably the most valuable guy. But I'd put Albert Pujols right behind Barry.

—MANAGER TONY LARUSSA

Everything he hit was really blessed. He could break bones with his shots. Blindfold me and I could still tell you when Joe hit the ball. It had a special crack.

—ERNIE SHORE

If ever anyone wielded a blunt instrument at home plate, it was Harmon Killebrew. There was nothing subtle about the Idaho strongboy and it was always his intention to mash a pitched ball as hard and as far as he could.

—DONALD HONIG

Walter Johnson's got a gun concealed about his person. They can't tell me he throws them balls with his arm.

—RING LARDNER

Jeter is a six-tool player. I've never eaten with him so I can't tell you if he has good table manners, but I would imagine he has those too.

—JOHNNY OATES

When Satchel Paige wound up to pitch, he looked like a cross between Ichabod Crane and Rip Van Winkle. He was easy to imitate and funny to watch, unless you were the batter trying to hit against him.

—AL HIRSHBERG

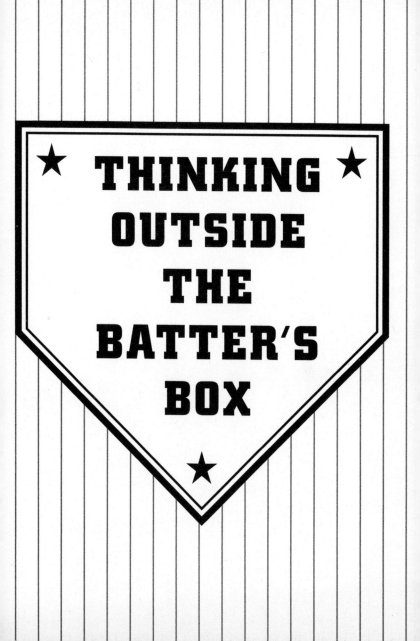

BASEBALL PROVIDES so many opportunities to revel in victory, cry in defeat, and reminisce on heroes gone past. But what really makes baseball special is how readily it lends itself to philosophical thought. Players, managers, writers, and even the most casual fans are capable of harnessing some bit of baseball's magic to create some beauty of their own.

You see, the Mets are losers, just like nearly everybody else in life. This is a team for the cab driver who gets held up and the guy who loses out on a promotion because he didn't maneuver himself to lunch with the boss enough. It is the team for every guy who has to get out of bed in the morning and go to work for short money on a job he does not like. And it is the team for every woman who looks up ten years later and sees her husband eating dinner in a t-shirt and wonders how the hell she ever let this guy talk her into getting married. The Yankees? Who does well enough to root for them, Laurence Rockefeller?

—JIMMY BRESLIN

Yesterday's home runs don't win today's games.

—BABE RUTH

It's the mathematical potential for a single game to last forever, in a suspended world where no clock rules the day, that aligns baseball as much with the dead as the living.

—BILL VAUGHN

Every day is a new opportunity. You can build on yesterday's success or put its failures behind and start over again. That's the way life is, with a new game every day, and that's the way baseball is.

—BOB FELLER

That moment, when you first lay eyes on that field—The Monster, the triangle, the scoreboard, the light tower Big Mac bashed, the left-field grass where Ted (Williams) once roamed—it all defines to me why baseball is such a magical game.

—JAYSON STARK

It is the life-affirming genius of baseball that the short can pummel the tall, the rotund can make fools of the sleek, and no matter how far down you find yourself in the bottom of the ninth you can always pull out a miracle.

—BILL VAUGHN

More than any other American sport, baseball creates the magnetic, addictive illusion that it can almost be understood.

—THOMAS BOSWELL

As I grew up, I knew that as a building (Fenway Park) was on the level of Mount Olympus, the Pyramid at Giza, the nation's capital, the czar's Winter Palace, and the Louvre —except, of course, that is better than all those inconsequential places.

—BART GIAMATTI

Most people, ordinary citizens, regard Major League Baseball with a reverence bordering on foolishness. They believe an institution so old and storied must be honest at its core. Even after the '94 strike, even after steroids, they continue to believe. Baseball is the drunken uncle America keeps inviting back to Thanksgiving, even though we know he's going to puke and pass out on the floor.

—T.T. MONDAY

That's why baseball is more like life than other games. Sometimes I feel like that's all I do in life, keep track of my errors.

—MICHAEL CHABON

Baseball has so much history and tradition. You can respect it, or you can exploit it for profit, but it's still being made all over the place, all the time.

—MICHAEL LEWIS

The great thing about baseball is, I've heard a hundred statements beginning, "The great thing about baseball is…"

—JON SINDELL

Ninety feet between bases is perhaps as close as man has ever come to perfection.

—RED SMITH

A team is where a boy can prove his courage on his own. A gang is where a coward goes to hide.

—MICKEY MANTLE

A pitcher will never be a big winner until he hates hitters.

—EARLY WYNN

Every day is a new opportunity. You can build on yesterday's success or put its failures behind and start over again.

—BOB FELLER

Progress always involves risks. You can't steal second base and keep your foot on first.

—FREDERICK B. WILCOX

One of the beautiful things about baseball is that every once in a while you have to reach down and prove something.

—NOLAN RYAN

To me, baseball has always been a reflection of life. Like life, it adjusts. It survives everything.

—WILLIE STARGELL

You spend a good piece of your life gripping a baseball, and in the end it turns out that it was the other way around.

—Jim Bouton

I don't think I can get into my deep inner thoughts about hitting. It's like talking about religion.

—Mike Schmidt

Knowing the strike zone is very important, but I think the first thing is knowing yourself, knowing what things you do well.

—Tony Gwynn

Everyone has something special and unique. But if you don't let anyone see it, it just gets wasted. It goes to the grave.

—RICH HILL

Make sure your worst enemy doesn't live between your ears. Self-doubt kills dreams. You are more capable than you think.

—KRIS BRYANT

Selfishness is the root of all evil in sports. When you're only looking out for yourself, bad things happen. It's about the team.

—DAVID ROSS

Any time you have an opportunity to make a difference in this world and you don't, then you are wasting your time on Earth.

—ROBERTO CLEMENTE

You must try to generate happiness within yourself. If you aren't happy in one place, chances are you won't be happy anyplace.

—ERNIE BANKS

It doesn't matter if we were down 3-0. You've just got to keep the faith. The game is not over until the last out.

—DAVID ORTIZ

The ballplayer who loses his head, who can't keep his cool, is worse than no ballplayer at all.

—LOU GEHRIG

You gotta be a man to play baseball for a living, but you gotta have a lot of little boy in you, too.

—ROY CAMPANELLA

It never ceases to amaze me how many of baseball's wounds are self-inflicted.

—BILL VEECK

Life will throw you curves, just keep fouling them off. The right pitch will come, and when it does, be ready to run the bases.

—RICK MAKSIAN

Baseball is drama with an endless run and an ever-changing cast.

—JOE GARAGIOLA

Some people are born on third base and go through life thinking they hit a triple.

—BARRY SWITZER

I've come to the conclusion that the two most important things in life are good friends and a good bullpen.

—BOB LEMON

Baseball? It's just a game, as simple as a ball and a bat. Yet, as complex as the American spirit it symbolizes.

—ERNIE HARWELL

You don't save a pitcher for tomorrow. Tomorrow it may rain.

—LEO DUROCHER

There are so many people who tell you that you can't. What you've got to do is turn around and say, "Watch me".

—BRYCE HARPER

What you lack in talent can be made up with desire, hustle, and giving 110% all the time.

—DON ZIMMER

Baseball has a way of humbling you. You can go 5-5 one day and 0-5 the next. It has a way of bringing you back down to earth.

—CHIPPER JONES

When you're in a slump, it's almost as if you look out at the field and it's one big glove.

—VANCE LAW

Pressure is a word that is misused. When you start thinking of pressure, it's because you've started to think of failure.

—TOMMY LASORDA

Maximum effort and hustle on every play are two things that require zero athletic ability.

—WADE BOGGS

It's unbelievable how much you don't know about the game you've been playing all your life.

—MICKEY MANTLE

Consistency is something you can always improve on. You can always be more consistent with your mental approach.

—GREG MADDUX

It isn't hard to be good from time to time in sports. What is tough, is being good every day.

—WILLIE MAYS

Experience is a hard teacher because she gives the test first, the lesson afterward.

—VERNON LAW

The more pitches you see, the more dangerous you become.

—HAWK HARRELSON

Never permit the pressure to exceed the pleasure of playing this game.

—JOE MADDON

Always follow your dreams, don't let anyone tell you that you can't be something.

—Alex Rodriguez

A life is not important except in the impact it has on other lives.

—Jackie Robinson

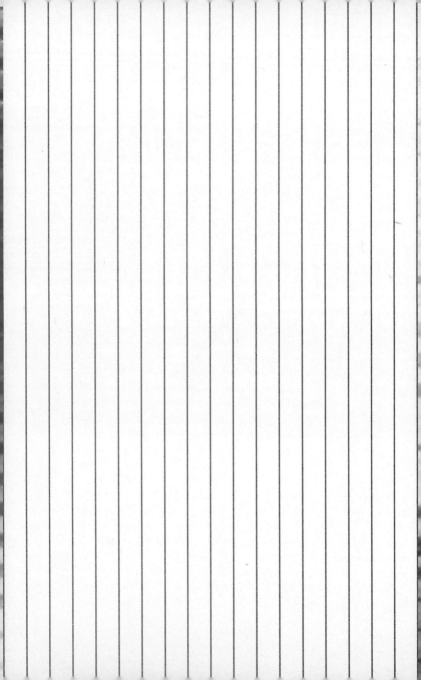